AMAZING MACHINES

A TONY MITTON TREASURY
ILLUSTRATED BY ANT PARKER

KINGFISHER
a Houghton Mifflin Company imprint
222 Berkeley Street
Boston, Massachusetts 02116
www.houghtonmifflinbooks.com

First published in this format in 2005
10 9 8 7 6 5 4 3 2 1

The material in this collection was first published by Kingfisher
in eight separate volumes:
Dazzling Diggers (1997)
Roaring Rockets (1997)
Flashing Fire Engines (1998)
Terrific Trains (1998)
Amazing Airplanes (2002)
Busy Boats (2002)
Tough Trucks (2003)
Tremendous Tractors (2003)

ISBN 0-7534-5938-8
ISBN 978-07534-5938-6

Printed in China

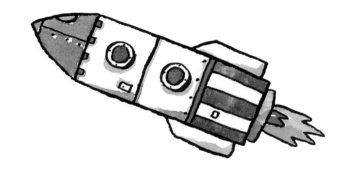

AMAZING
MACHINES

A TONY MITTON TREASURY
ILLUSTRATED BY ANT PARKER

KINGFISHER

BOSTON

Contents

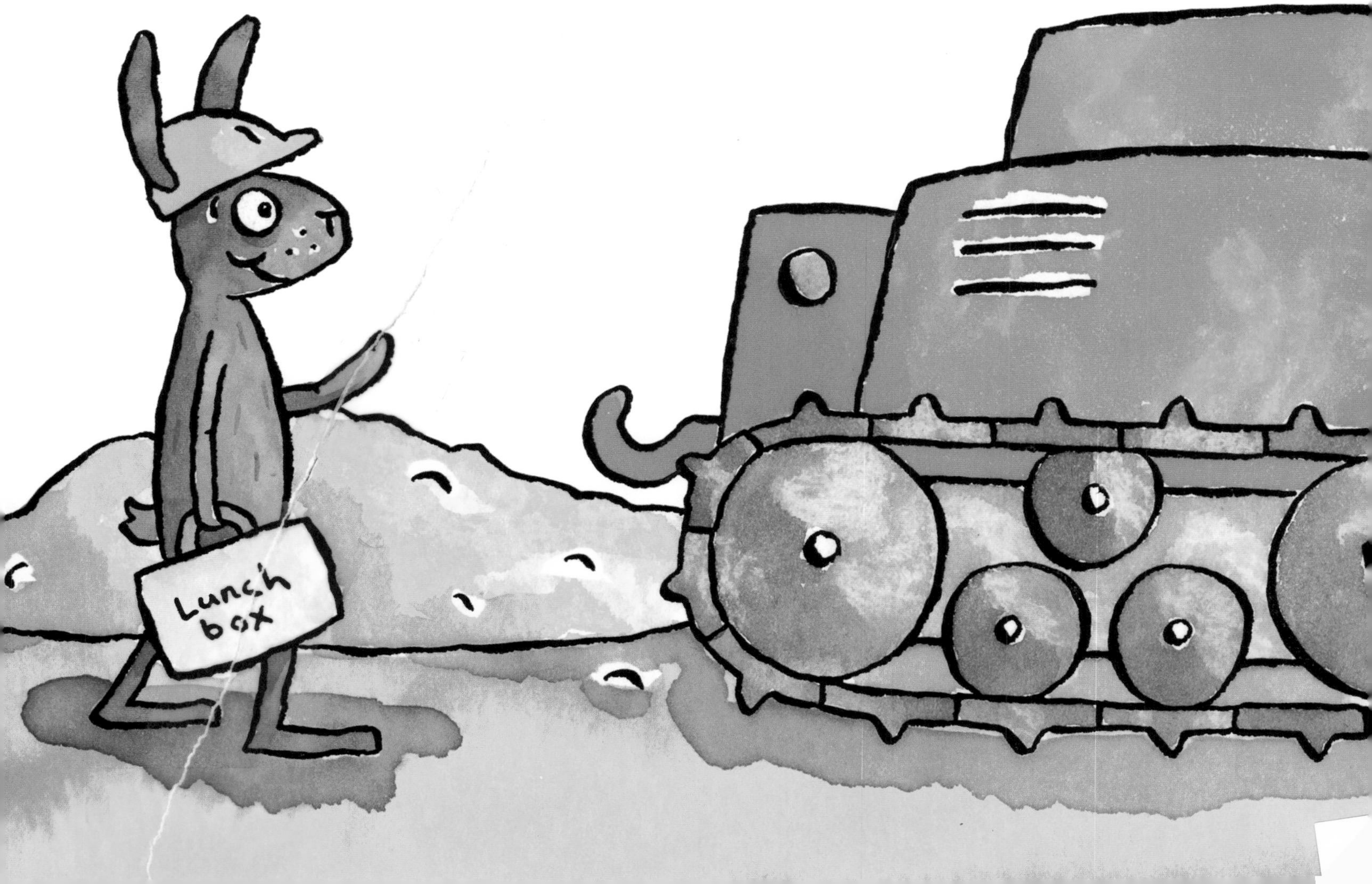
Lunch box

Amazing
AIRPLANES

Whoosh

An airplane is amazing,
for it travels through the sky,

12

above the clouds for miles and miles,
so very fast and high!

13

An airport is the place you go
to take a trip by air.

You check in at the terminal to show
you've paid your fare.

The ground crew weigh your luggage
and load it in the hold.

And then you take the walkway to the plane
when you are told.

The flight deck's where the captain
and copilot do their jobs.
They both know how to fly the plane
with all its dials and knobs.

They radio Control Tower to check
the runway's clear.
They can't take off unless it is,
with other planes so near.

By intercom the captain on the flight deck
says hello.

You have to put your seat belt on
before the plane can go!

A plane is big and heavy,
yet it climbs up really high.

22

It zooms along the runway
and soars into the sky.

23

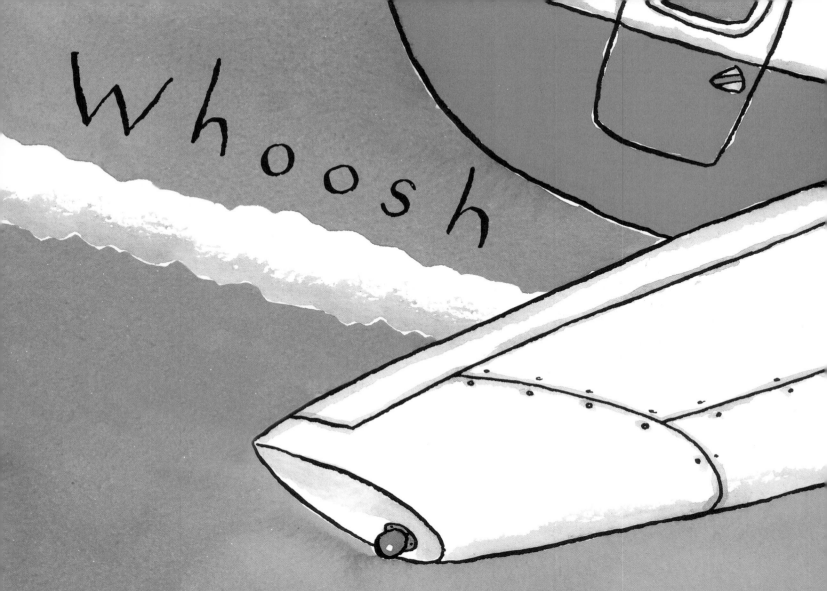

Its wings hold big jet engines,
which are loud and very strong.
They suck in air and blow it through
to whoosh the plane along.

24

When the plane moves fast enough,
the air around's so swift
it pushes up beneath the wings
and makes the whole plane lift.

Soon the plane is in the air,
so now you're on your flight.
The cabin crew look after you
and make sure you're all right.

26

They bring you drinks and magazines
and trays of food to eat.
And sometimes there's a movie
you can watch while in your seat.

27

When the journey's over,
the captain lands the plane.
Control Tower has to say it's safe
for coming down again.

You sit with seat belt fastened,
there's a bumpy, rumbling sound—
the wheels are making contact,
and the plane is on the ground!

29

At last the doors are opening.
Then out you come with smiles.

So give a cheer. Hooray—you're here!
You've flown for miles and miles.

31

Airplane parts

control tower
from here the air traffic controllers direct the planes and tell pilots when to take off and land safely

flight deck
sometimes called the **cockpit** this is where the pilot and copilot sit

wheel
the wheels fold away while the plane is in the air

hold
this is the space where heavy luggage is stored

wing →
the wings are hollow to make them as light as possible and a smooth shape so they move through the air easily

jet engine
jet engines blow out air and gas to push the plane forward—the gas is made by burning fuel

terminal
this is the building at the airport where passengers go to catch a plane

TERMINAL

Boats are really wonderful for sailing us around.
They travel through the water
with a sloppy-slappy sound.

34

It's fun to go out boating, especially in the sun.
The water's cool and sparkly,
so come on, everyone!

35

A boat sits on the water
like an empty bowl or cup.
It's hollow and it's full of air,
and that's what keeps it up.

An anchor holds you steady
when you're bobbing in a bay.
You wind a chain to raise it
when you want to sail away.

Over lakes and seas and rivers,
wind blows very strong.
Some boats have sails to catch it
so it pushes them along.

38

To handle boats with masts and sails,
you need a clever crew.
The captain is the one in charge,
who tells them what to do.

A dinghy or a rowboat
is useful near the shore.

You make it travel backward
by pulling on each oar.

A motorboat is powered
by propeller from the back.
It whooshes through the water
and leaves a foamy track.

And just in case, by accident,
you tumble from the boat,
you have to wear a life jacket,
made to help you float.

Some boats are built for fishing
where the ocean waves are steep.

44

Their nets are cast to catch the fish,
then haul them from the deep.

A ship can carry cargo,
which is loaded at the docks.

Heave ho! Look out below!
Here comes a giant box.

A ferry carries cars and trucks
to where they need to go.

The people travel up above.
The vehicles stay below.

49

A mighty ocean liner
has a big and busy crew.
It carries many passengers.
They're waving now. Yoo-hoo!

50

The ship has cozy cabins
where the passengers can stay.
And out on deck they stroll around
and watch the sea or play.

51

But when the journey's over—
Ahoy! The lighthouse rock!

The ship glides into harbor
and ties up at the dock.

53

Boat parts

lighthouse

this is a tall building on the coast with a flashing light to guide ships and keep them away from rocks

anchor

this is a very heavy piece of metal with hooks that dig into the ground under the water and stop the boat from drifting away

propeller

this has **blades** that spin around very fast at the back of the boat and push against the water to move the boat forward

oars

these are long poles with flat **blades** on the end that push against the water to move the boat forward

deck

this is the floor of a boat

cabin

this is the little room where you sleep on board a boat

cargo

this is the name for the goods that a ship carries

name

many boats are given names by their owners

MANDY

FRAGILE

Dazzling DIGGERS

Diggers are noisy, strong, and big.

Diggers can carry and push and dig.

Diggers have shovels to scoop and lift,

Scrunch

blades that bulldoze, shunt, and shift.

Diggers have buckets to gouge out ground,

breakers that crack and smash and pound.

Diggers move rubble and rocks and soil,

so diggers need drinks of diesel oil.

Some have tires and some have tracks.

Some keep steady with legs called jacks.

Tires and tracks grip hard as they travel,

squish through mud and grind through gravel.

Diggers go scrunch and squelch and slosh.

This dirty digger needs a really good wash.

Diggers can bash and crash and break,

make things crumble, shiver, and shake.

Diggers can heave and hoist and haul.

Diggers help buildings tower up tall.

73

Drivers park neatly, down on the site.

And then they all go home. Goodnight!

Digger parts

levers

these control different parts of the digger

tire

this helps the wheel to grip the ground and get the digger moving

bucket

this is for digging and scooping out

jack

this holds the digger steady when it is lifting or digging

breaker

this is for cracking concrete or lumps of rock

piston

this is a strong pump that makes parts of the digger move around

blade

this is for knocking down and pushing along

tracks

these help the digger to travel over slippery or bumpy ground

Flashing
FIRE ENGINES

Big, bold fire engines, waiting day and night,

ready for a rescue or a blazing fire to fight.

As soon as there's a fire alarm,
the engine starts to roar.

The firefighters jump aboard—
it rumbles out the door.

Watch the engine speeding, on its daring dash.

Hear its siren screaming. See its bright lights flash.

In helmets, fireproof pants and jackets,
boots so big and strong,

the crew is dressed and ready
as the engine zooms along.

When the engine finds the fire,
it quickly pulls up near.

The crew jumps out, unrolls the hose,
and gets out all the gear.

The hose points up its nozzle
and shoots a jet of spray.
It squirts right at the blazing flames
and sizzles them away.

88

The water tank is empty soon,
so where can more be found?
The engine's pump can pull it up
from pipes below the ground.

The fire is hot and roaring.
It makes a lot of smoke.

The firefighters put on masks,
otherwise they'd choke.

The ladder rises upward. It reaches for the sky.
A fire engine's ladder stretches up so very high!

Sometimes there's a platform, right up at the top.
It waits beside the window. Then into it you hop.

At last the fire's extinguished.
The flames are all put out.

plop!

plop!

Lower the ladder. Roll the hose.
"Hurray!" the fire crew shouts.

Back inside the station,
the crew can take a break.

But the fire engine's ready
and it's waiting wide-awake.

Fire Engine parts

helmet

this is a hard hat that protects the firefighter's head

Fireproof pants and Jackets

these are made from special material that does not burn easily and protects firefighters from the fire

masks and tank

we cannot breathe in smoky air, so firefighters carry clean air in **tanks** on their backs. The air flows into their **masks**

siren

this makes a loud noise to tell people to move out of the way and let the fire engine pass

water tank

this is inside the middle of the fire engine and holds water to fight the fire—some fire engines carry foam, too

pump

this sucks water from the tank and pushes it out throug huge **hoses**. The pump can also get water from a **hydrant** attached to underground pipe

hose connects to **pump**

Roaring ROCKETS

Rockets have power. They rise and roar.

This rocket's waiting, ready to soar.

Rockets carry astronauts with cool white suits,

oxygen helmets, and gravity boots.

The countdown is finishing: 3, 2, 1 . . .

Action! Blast off! The journey's begun.

Rockets have fuel in great big tanks.

When they are empty, they drop away . . . thanks!

Up in space you're really light,
108

so astronauts need to buckle up tight.

Rockets go far. Through space they zoom,

reaching as far as the big, round moon.

Down comes the lander with legs out ready

and fiery boosters to hold it steady.

Out come the astronauts to plant their flag

and scoop up samples in their moon-rock bag.

115

Rockets explore. Through space they roam.

But when they're done, they head back home.

Rockets re-enter in a fiery flash,
to land in the sea with a sizzling splash!

The helicopter carries the brave crew away.
Three cheers for the astronauts:
Hip! Hip! Hooray!

Rocket parts

gravity boots

gravity keeps us on the ground but there is not a lot of gravity on the moon, so astronauts wear these boots to stop them floating away

lunar lander

Lunar lander

this takes astronauts down from the rocket to land on the moon

oxygen helmet

we need to breathe oxygen but there isn't any in space, so astronauts carry their own supply which flows into their helmets

fuel tanks

these hold the fuel that makes the rocket go

command module

this is where the astronauts live on their way to and from the moon

Terrific
TRAINS

Big trains, small trains, old trains and new,

rattling and whistling—Choo, Choo, Choo!

Starting from the station with a whistle and a hiss.

steam trains huffing and puffing like this.

Whoosh!

Diesel trains rushing as they rattle down the line,

126

...warning us they're coming with a long, low whine.

Metal wheels whirl as they whizz along the track.
They shimmer and they swish
with a slick click-clack.

Coaches are coupled in a neat, long chain.
An engine pulls the coaches,
and that makes a train.

If a train meets a river or a valley or a ridge,

the coaches rumble over on a big, strong bridge.

If a train meets a mountain it doesn't have to stop

It travels through a tunnel and your ears go pop!

When too many trains try to share the same track

he signals and the switches have to hold some back.

When the rail meets a road,
there's a crossing with a gate.

The train rushes through
while the traffic has to wait.

Trains travel anytime, even very late.

This train's delivering a big load of freight.

This train's for passengers,
it's ready at the station.

All aboard and wave goodbye—
we're going on vacation!

Train parts

rails

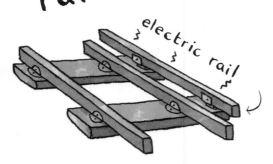

electric rail

these are metal strips that form a pathway called a **track** or **railroad line**. Some trains get their power from an electric rail

whistle

this makes a noise to warn everyone that the train is coming

freight car

this is for carrying goods, called **freight**

signal

this tells engineers when to stop and go

coach

this is for carrying people, called **passengers**

switches

these are the short rails that move to let a train switch from one track to another

Tough TRUCKS

rumble

Trucks are tough and sturdy.
They take on heavy loads,

then thunder on their giant tires
down long and busy roads.

All trucks have a cab up front.
The driver sits inside.
The truck's controls are all around,
ready for the ride.

The driver starts the engine
and, when the way is clear,
accelerates along the road
and turns the wheel to steer.

147

Some truck cabs have a bunk bed,
a curtain, and a light

to make a tiny bedroom
where the driver sleeps at night.

A big rig has a semitrailer
fitted with a pin.
Its tractor unit has a slot
to click the trailer in.

So when the rig is traveling
on roads that weave and wend,
the separate parts turn one by one
to get around a bend.

151

A garbage truck collects the trash,
grumbling down the street.

152

It lifts the cans and empties them
to keep things clean and neat.

A concrete mixer stirs its load
while traveling to the site.
The foreman points, "Just pour it here.
We're ready now. Alright?"

The piston on a dump truck
can push to tilt it up.
We're just about to tip some rubble.
Ready, steady, hup!

155

A tanker carries liquids,
so it's sealed up good and tight.

This shiny tanker's full of milk,
all creamy, cool, and white.

When traveling long distances,
you're on the road alone,
so drivers keep in touch
by CB radio or phone.

This truck has had a breakdown,
but the driver didn't panic.
He radioed around and found
a handy truck mechanic.

Driving trucks is tiring,
but you need to be awake.

So drivers park at truck stops
for a meal or a break.

But look, we've reached the depot.
We've made another run.

The forklift starts unloading,
and the foreman shouts, "Well done!"

Truck parts

tractor-trailer

this is made up of a tractor and a semitrailer—
it is also called a **semi** or a **big rig**

cab

this is where the driver sits

semitrailer

this holds the truck's load

tractor

this pulls the trailer

CB radio

a driver can use this special
radio to talk to other drivers

piston

also called a **hoist**, this is
a strong pump that pushes
up the back of a dump
truck to help it tip
its load

Tremendous
TRACTORS

Tremendous, chuggy tractors,
so sturdy and so strong,

hitching up to farm machines
and pulling them along.

Their big black tires have solid treads
that help them not to slip.
These chunky treads can chew the ground
and get the wheels to grip.

A tractor works on farmland,
so its body must be tough.
It sits high up above the ground,
for farmland can be rough.

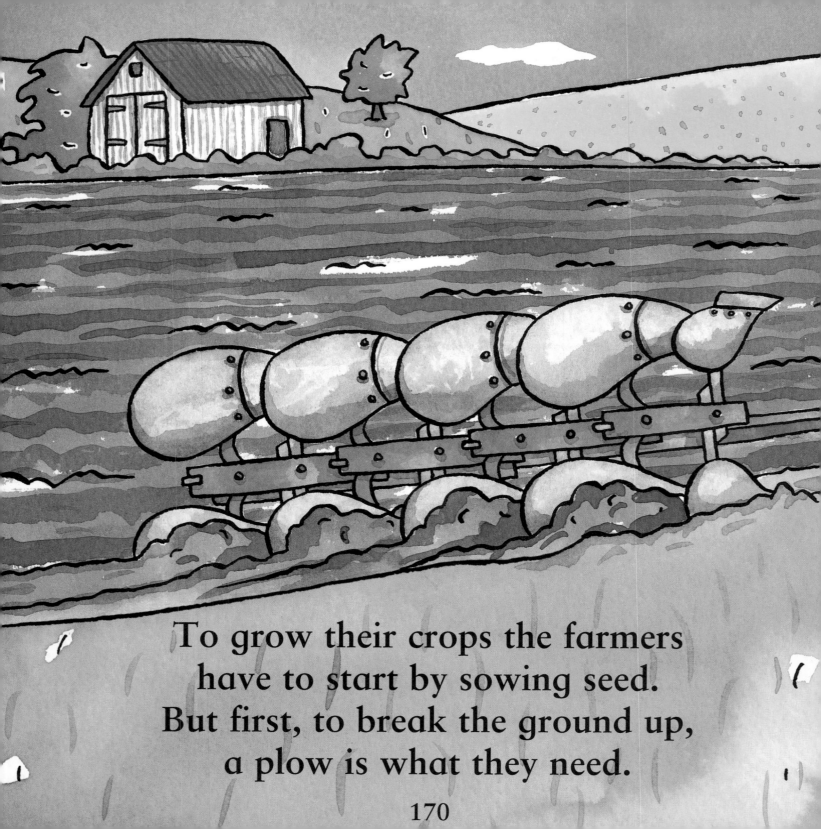

To grow their crops the farmers
have to start by sowing seed.
But first, to break the ground up,
a plow is what they need.

A tractor pulls the plow
across the field, up and down.
The plow blades cut the soil
into furrows, rich and brown.

crumble

crunch

The tractor hauls the harrow next
to break the soil some more.

Disk harrows crush the clods up—
that's what a harrow's for.

It's time to use the roller now,
a tube that rolls around

174

for flattening the field,
pushing stones beneath the ground.

The seed drill has a hopper,
a seed box that you fill.
When it's time for planting,
the tractor pulls the drill.

The seed drill makes a row of grooves
in which the seeds can drop.
The spikes then rake a covering of
soil across the top.

177

chop
chop
chop

When a hay crop's fully grown,
the mower comes and mows.

178

It cuts the grass and
leaves it out to dry in tidy rows.

Later on a baler scoops
the stalks up from the ground
and shapes them into bales,
which are bundles, square or round.

A bale of hay is heavy,
so it's very hard to lift.
A bale fork on a tractor
makes it easier to shift.

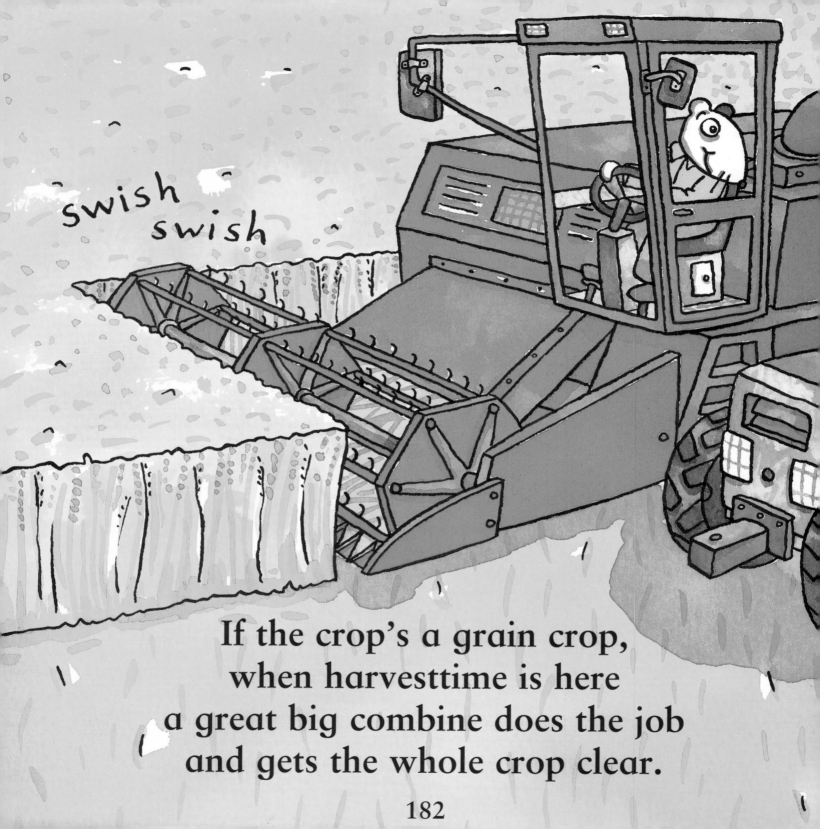

swish
swish

If the crop's a grain crop,
when harvesttime is here
a great big combine does the job
and gets the whole crop clear.

It cuts the stalks and threshes them
to knock the grain all out,
then spreads the straw behind it
as the grain spills from the spout.

183

A tractor with a trailer
shifts bales of straw or hay,
takes food to hungry animals,
or carries crops away.

The tractor and the farmer
work hard and do their best.
So when the day is over,
they both deserve a rest.

Tractor parts

tire
this has chunky **treads** to help the wheel grip bumpy or slippery ground

seed drill
this scratches small grooves in the ground for planting seeds

← **hopper**
this holds the seeds and blows them out through a row of tubes

bale fork
this is for lifting bales of hay or straw and moving them around

blade

a plow has sharp blades, or **shares,** to cut into the ground and turn over the soil

spikes
these move through the ground to cover the seeds after they drop